Sue currently works in the retail health industry having previously worked for the NHS. She always enjoyed writing poetry. She currently lives in Leicestershire with her husband and king, Charles Spaniel.

She has four children, two step sons and six grandchildren, and loves spending time with them all. In her spare time, Sue enjoys walking, reading, writing, theatre, eating out and word puzzles.

These poems are dedicated to my lovely grandma for always being there for me. To my parents, who became people to me as I got older, for always trying their best. Also I want to dedicate them to my wonderful daughters, son, stepsons, and grandchildren, who always have made me proud, and still continue to do so. Lacey and Alfie, who share my passion for writing. To my husband for his ongoing support, and always believing I could do this. To Peter Unwin, my guardian angel social-worker, who ensured my baby son and I had a home.

These poems are also for all you lovely people out there who recognise the struggles and joys of everyday life, and the magic of children.

Sue Batchelor

TIGHTROPE

AUSTIN MACAULEY PUBLISHERS™

LONDON • CAMBRIDGE • NEW YORK • SHARJAH

A CIP catalogue record for this title is available from the British
Library.

ISBN 9781528996143 (Paperback)
ISBN 9781528996150 (Hardback)
ISBN 9781528996167 (ePub e-book)

www.austinmacauley.com

First Published (2020)
Austin Macauley Publishers Ltd
25 Canada Square
Canary Wharf
London
E14 5LQ

I want to say thank you to my husband, Malc, for all his love and support. For listening to my poems and always believing in me and helping me to believe in myself. The love and support I always get from my family pushes me forward in anything I set out to achieve. I am lucky that I have such a wonderful supportive family to write about.

I want to thank Austin Macauley Publishers for their help in designing my book cover and getting my book out there, and to my niece, Claire, for the lovely photograph.

A Date with Fate!

Why is it life can be so cruel?
Without a pattern or a rule.
There is no sense to many things
With all the heartache that it brings.

Is it by chance, or is it fate?
That you were standing by that gate?
Had you been there the day before
Would you be here? I'm not so sure!

Is it the time? Is it the place?
Or who is standing in that space?
Where death or trauma will occur!
Does it depend on where you were!

Or does it matter where you are?
If you have travelled near or far!
Or is it just a case of fate?
I'll change my plans! No, it's too late!

A World of Tissues

We're in the car and on our way
A busy morning, start of day.
With people dashing everywhere
Young mums and tots take extra care.

We drive along the busy street
A child is fastened in his seat.
Mum grabs a tissue, wipes his nose
Under the car the tissue goes.

You are such a great example!
Your one tissue just a sample.
Each one of us could take one too
Dispose of it the way you do.

Each day one more snotty tissue
No big deal, so what's the issue?
Four hundred people in your street
All throw a tissue, what a treat.

That's lots of tissues in a year
You may just think, 'So what's to fear?'
I see a paper mâché world
Made from the tissues you have hurled.

Yes, paper mâché, from the rain
The snot's the glue, what's to explain.
By the way I will just mention
Thoughtlessness without intention.

Just stop and think before you throw
'Oh, where will all my litter go.'
You know it is a choice for you
Think paper mâché on your shoe.

The drive to work is now so slow
Is that because you're stuck in snow?
Not to worry, no big deal.
OH NO! There's snotters on my wheel!

After the Holiday

And so, I knew I couldn't win
I chose to quit and just gave in.
They call it justice but it's not
It's all part of a twisted plot.

You start to question your own mind
Was I mistaken, was I blind?
Was I confused? Was I asleep?
Perhaps just lightly. Maybe deep.

The summer dress I chose to wear
With yellow flowers, shoulders bare.
I felt so pretty young and free
I sensed my neighbour's eyes on me.

A holiday with lots of sun
The five of us had so much fun.
My friend and I, our children too
The yellow sand and sea of blue.

He said, "Hello, I want you Sue."
I blinked my eyes. A voice I knew.
The silhouette was still and tall
So scared, I couldn't move at all.

I saw his face. I said his name
I asked myself was I to blame.
I felt so frightened but kept calm
Did he intend to do us harm.

My children sleeping nearby
Not wanting them to wake and cry.
And later came the morning light
I'd somehow made it through the night.

The window had been forced they said
His entry point up to my bed.
These friends I had lived just next door
His wife told me I was a whore.

The police asked did I tell him no
Of course. I wanted him to go.
The smell of beer filled the air
I couldn't move. I didn't dare.

I dropped the case. I wouldn't win
Despite the fact that he broke in.
I said I didn't try to fight
Whilst frozen in a state of fright.

So glad my children didn't wake
Their innocence he didn't take.
I knew he could be volatile
My babies woke up with a smile.

Aramis and Steve

Steve, Aramis is your best friend
You know on him you can depend.
He's faithful and he's always there
His loyalty you can't compare.

You care for him, he knows you do
He always wants to be with you.
He waits for you till you get home
You take him out, and off you roam.

Two friends together, having fun
Man and dog, till day is done.
That sort of loyalty is rare
He waits for you, he's always there.

Baker Street

A lady came in every day
With eggs and sausage in a tray.
I cooked it and was very glad
To know each day a meal I'd had.

That song again! It's Baker Street!
Reminds me of my breakfast treat.
I see the kitchen. Feel the sun
My independence had begun.

A bedsit for my son and me
A single mum. It's so lonely.
I was so lucky. Had a place.
Somewhere to sleep. A home. A base.

I had some help. I kept my boy.
I was his mum. He brought me joy.
And Peter Unwin, you were king
You took me under your great wing.

Onto the ward you came to me
As warm and kind as you could be.
You took me shopping – baby things
With all the pleasure that it brings.

Without you where would I be now
So Peter, won't you take a bow.
The scared young girl I used to be
Has gone because you rescued me.

Without you what would I have done
I'm lucky that I kept my son.
I hate to think what might have been
My baby gone! A broken teen!

I feel the pain. A mother's plight
To find her child and re-unite.
An adult now, it's hard to say
"I'm sorry I gave you away.

"I love you and I thought of you
Every day my whole life through
I hugged you and then you were gone
I cried and somehow carried on."

I kept you and I am so glad
For all the joy that I have had
On tele Long Lost Family
I am so glad that wasn't me!

Blowing in the Wind

Stay awhile, I wish I'd said
I wanted him to see me wed.
Just eight months it was so near
He didn't think he'd still be here.

It's sixteen years ago today
Since my sweet father went away.
He couldn't wait, he had to go
But why just then we'll never know.

He was so tired, so ill and thin
We knew this time he wouldn't win.
He looked at me as if he knew
And then he said, "I've had it Sue."

What could I say, I couldn't lie
We both knew that my dad would die.
I looked at him, he looked at me
The plain acceptance I could see.

I let him down, I didn't speak
I felt deflated and so weak.
He spoke about the days gone by
I saw the glinting in his eye.

He wasn't scared in those last days
He spoke of green grass in the haze.
With eyes looking up, he talked to me
Describing all that he could see.

He saw a field of grass so green
A place he thinks he might have been.
He sees a bike of forties era
Racing along and getting nearer.

"He looks like Biggles all in leather."
"He's racing along, it's lovely weather."
"It's windy and his scarf is blowing."
I look at Dad, his face is glowing.

I watch my dad, I love him so
I think he knows it's time to go.
He describes this man, he's full of joy
He reminds me of a little boy.

"It looks so lovely, I feel so free."
I don't think he's aware of me.
"Beautiful fields are all I see
I look across, he's beckoning me."

This final time I sat with Dad
Was so special it made me glad
That he had shared such joy with me
Describing things so vividly.

He went to sleep, I tiptoed out
He wasn't scared, I had no doubt.
His face had been so full of joy
He looked just like a little boy.

I picture my dad now he's not here.
I see the man in the forties gear.
I feel the wind. I see the sun.
He's on that bike. He's having fun!

Boo!

I must be doing this for a reason
Oh yes, I forgot! Boo is in season.
I have a nappy and a pad
So what can really be so bad?

Come here please! Just sit still!
I keep grabbing her until
I can fix the pad in place
And now the Velcro, it's a race.

Boo twists around, the Velcro sticks
To the floor we're in a fix.
Got her now, so hold her tight
I pin her down with all my might.

The pad is on! Oh no, it's not!
Not really sure which bit I've got.
Oh, that's her head, now where's her bum!
Just need the Velcro around her tum!

She's sitting still, let's get it done
I've got her now, so she can't run.
Velcro done, now I can't fail
Oh, bloody hell, I've lost her tail!!

Boxes

And now it's time to take them down
I make a start but wear a frown.
I'm in no rush, I'll take my time
I'm closing down this pantomime.

I think about the fun we've had
I miss all that, it makes me sad.
We got together, had some wine
This time of year, a love of mine.

The sparkles, glitter and the joy
The pleasure of a parcelled toy.
The chatter, laughter ringing out
Now this is what it's all about.

It's quiet now. The laughs subside.
Thoughts old and new dance and collide.
I take a bauble shining bright
I wrap it up and fold it tight.

Each one special in its glory
Festive but it tells a story.
The boxes now begin to fill
With all their secrets held until.

December comes and they'll come out
To brighten up the house throughout.
The tree is bare. I speak to it
"You're special even when unlit."

Things may have changed the next time round
Will you be standing on this ground?
When you emerge what will you see?
This room but painted differently?

A different house, another view?
Whatever's new we'll still have you.
You've served us well, stood proud and strong
You'll stay with us where you belong.

Carma

Our cleaning lady is the best
She treats us as a welcome guest.
She has a chat, and shares a joke
Smiles at all the holiday folk.

Her trolley piled high with linen
Her morning shift is just beginning.
We see her in the corridor
She starts to clean on the third floor.

Carma you are such a treasure
To see your face is such a pleasure.
You work so hard, you always smile
And still take time to talk a while.

Center Parcs

So Center Parcs, our yearly treat
Where Bache and Batch drive up and meet.
A festive latte starts the hol
So one for Malc, Nick, me and Poll.

And now our Christmas time will start
This wonderland is in our heart.
With Christmas trees and lots of snow
Illuminations make us glow.

As we wind down, we have a wine
And look at all the trees of pine.
As we walk out, we understand
Our need to have this wonderland.

Our yearly catch-up brings such glee
An update for my sis and me.
The boys trudge on. We lag behind
We chatter as we both unwind.

It's nice and cold, the sun is out
It's winter now there is no doubt.
So put the mulled wine on to heat
A lovely little Christmas treat.

As we head out, mulled wine in hand
It's all lit up in wonderland.
The choir sings and fireworks start
A piece of heaven in my heart.

Chameleon

Costume change. Chameleon queen
The fiery reds to calming green.
The ice-cold glare, then laughing eyes
This quick-change artist loves surprise.

And her shoes, are they made from snake?
Can you tell if the skin is fake?
A keen eye would know that for sure
Would penetrate the cold false core.

Beware the beauty. Gentle grace
The pale complexion. Smooth soft face.
Those rounded words, precise and neat
Her laughter light. Melodic treat.

A reptile lurks inside this cat
With twisted words the venom's spat!
A vipers' tongue. The lethal sting.
You cry out. She won't feel a thing.

The cat returns, she's got the cream
Her twinkling eyes, a wide smug beam.
As sure as blood runs out and clots
This leopard will not change her spots!

Childhood

A single mum, it's very hard
Hoping your children don't get scarred.
By growing up without a dad
They're missing out, it makes me sad.

You try to do the best you can
And raise your kids without a man.
You don't know if you're doing right
You can't give up you have to fight.

You hide your pain, you hide your tears
Don't let your children know your fears.
You count the money while they play
To see how much we have today.

I'm feeling sad, I hope it clears
Growing stronger over the years.
The kids are happy, I'm feeling good
We got through this, I knew we would.

My babes are grown, they're doing well
Were they happy? It's hard to tell.
They talk of lovely times gone by
I did it well, it's time to cry.

Coffee

It doesn't matter what you say
Your body will give it away.
If there's a difference we will see
Which one spells out your honesty.

You look at me, a nervous smile
Before you speak you wait a while.
Saying it's great to have a chat
Next to each other we are sat.

The air is thick, we just don't gel
We want to leave we both can tell.
There is a silence, then a word
We speak together. Neither heard.

We start to squirm and then a grin
So choose a topic. Just begin.
The eye contact, a give away
As we both think of things to say.

With both arms folded and legs crossed
A summers day but still a frost.
Our body language does not lie
A clumsy hug! A quick goodbye!

Colours and Curves

Glad they took a great decision
Based upon a clear vision.
The Savoy Palace, 'poetic world'
Bold and curved a dream uncurled.

The inspiration all on show
Exuberance begins to glow.
Madeiran culture snapped inside
Embroidery the islands pride.

The furniture is made to measure
The wickerwork an age-old treasure.
With refined rooms of quality
Levadas, tunnels, history.

The furnished rooms of quality
A function room turns into three.
Eleven rooms make up the spa
A laurel forest spreading far.

The contours of the female shape
With animals who sit and drape
Just look and see the plants on view
The colours, curves, a dream comes true.

Confusion

Sometimes you feel like you could scream
You don't feel like you live the dream.
Things going wrong. The day seems long
Just help me out and hear my song.

I should do this! I must do that!
I'm eating more and getting fat!
I try to please! It doesn't work!
I'll run around and go berserk!

I am so tired! I'll go to bed!
Or shall I write or read instead?
So am I bored, or just fed up?
Where's the coffee. I'll have a cup.

I'm getting older. Is that why?
I am knackered. Time races by.
Indecision again this time
A poet but without a rhyme.

Connor

Connor was born the tenth of Jan
He would have been a fine young man.
When he was born, he was asleep
We knew he wasn't ours to keep.

The labour had been cruel and long
As nature played its tragic song.
You held your son and you were proud
The pride and sadness ringing loud.

Inside your womb he closed his eyes
A silent birth. No new born cries.
He was so handsome, thick dark hair
To lose him was so hard to bear.

His arms and legs were fine and strong
We didn't get to keep him long.
So bittersweet and yet surreal
The pain and love hard to conceal.

So keeping strong on that sad day
Not knowing what to do or say.
And later then you fell asleep
Exhausted with no son to keep.

A few days later I sat there
Outside the ward to sit and stare.
So many feelings well inside
To grieve is such a lonely ride.

Seven months pregnant you had bled
Doctor saying baby's dead.
A few days later you went in
So that your labour could begin.

So hard to watch you in such pain
The cruellest labour with no gain.
We held him. Sorrow mixed with pride.
This perfect boy you made inside.

A young mum robbed of nature's gift
I feel and think and then I drift.
It can't be real! How can it be!
I can't quite grasp reality!

Now twenty years have passed today
I talk to Connor as I pray.
I ask him if he is a man
Or is he still as he began.

Cotton Sheets

The crisp white sheets, so fresh and clean
Laundered and flat, the best I've seen.
The feel of cotton against my skin
I'm so relaxed as I slide in.

The whole apartment is so clean
I think about somewhere I've been.
The hospital where I had my son
Where motherhood had just begun.

So different then, I felt secure
So safe, so well, and so cared for.
The routine, such a daily treat
With cleaners buzzing round your feet.

Every morning, they were there
So out of bed, sit in the chair.
The sheets were changed, they mopped the floor
No chance for bad bugs to explore.

I felt so cared for and so clean
The cleanest place I'd ever been.
I loved the feeling of routine
Which at home I hadn't seen.

Dad Saw Red

We argued before our wedding day
Yes, the night before, I have to say!
Quite a bad omen, I know that now
More like bullying than a row.

I cannot remember what was said
I was crying, and we were in bed.
I was afraid and lay there awake
To marry him would be a mistake.

Why was I with him? I wish I knew
The day that he hit me was a clue.
That I should have left him there and then
before he could hurt me once again.

Reeling in shock, as Phil punched my face
I ran home screaming with him in chase.
I raced indoors, and my dad went wild!
Who up to now was kind and mild.

"Why did you hit her?" he calmly said
"She asked for it!" My dad shook his head.
Then out of the blue at such a pace
My dad made a fist and punched Phil's face!

Dodger

At six o'clock a year ago
We waited for the vet to show.
I'm sitting looking at the floor
Where Dodger lay a year before.

Nic had bought him a special treat
Sausages for Dodger to freely eat.
He ate them all. He looked so well
Was he happy? I couldn't tell.

The vet arrived, what would she say
I told her he seems good today.
She said his legs were pretty bad
She said he was a poorly lad.

She kneeled down, Dodge seemed to say
"Please help me take this pain away."
She shaved his leg. He lay so still.
He just lay there content until –

The very end, he seemed to know
It was his time. He had to go.
The needle entered with a prick
She told us it would be quite quick.

In Nic's loving arms Dodger lay
She held him till he passed away.
We made the choice, put Dodge to rest
We had to do what we thought best.

I know I used to get so mad –
At Dodge, and now I feel so bad.
He couldn't help it when he messed
I used to think he was a pest.

We had our times, I stroked his head
And always on my way to bed.
He looked so sad, so thin and small
And now he's in no pain at all.

You were a tinker, full of joy
A faithful and a handsome boy.
A guard dog and a loyal friend
You stayed with us until the end.

Don't Bring Them In

You rescued them, a heart of gold
You saw them and then said they're sold.
The cruel neglect they had before
The life they had is there no more.

A cold day and they wear their coats
A man whose time and love devotes.
He told me they were scared at first
The past with which they had been cursed.

You had a list of things to buy
We chatted and I asked you why…
Would someone want to do them harm
With all their beauty and that charm.

For years now they've had a home
Where they are loved and free to roam.
No longer do they live in fear
Instead a loving atmosphere.

To start with they had been unsure
If you would close and lock the door.
Where food and drink would never come
A cold, dark, loveless empty slum.

He'd brought his dogs inside the door
I'd thought what had he done that for.
This is a store and not a farm
Panic! Then a sense of calm.

A snowy day. A quiet shop
Gave me the time to smile and stop.
To really look at who I see
A person with a history.

So if you listen, you will find
A need to open up your mind.
We all have a different story
Sharing holds a key to glory.

Doop

Seven years ago today
A lovely baby came your way.
She changed your life, she made you whole
You loved her with your heart and soul.

A different Doop, a mumsy mum
This lovely girl grew in your tum.
It changed your world when she popped out
You loved her then, there is no doubt.

A little girl for you to hold
A pretty little pot of gold.
You were so wild, now so serene
The calmest you have ever been.

Your hormones changed, you were content
With baby who was heaven sent.
You were maternal through and through
Her name was Lacey. She changed you.

You have a very special bond
To last forever and beyond.
You love that girl, she loves you too
A job well done, I'm proud of you.

Ellistown

I really do love Ellistown
I looked at you and saw you frown.
You said, "It is a long commute."
I said, "Look at a different route."

We parked the car and looked around
It was so quiet, not a sound.
Lots of homes so small and neat
The rain is falling at our feet.

To see a new place, you must first
See it when it's at its worst.
If you like it when it's grey
You will love it on a fine day.

Aldi and Lidl weren't far away
Just down the road, I heard you say.
A shopping centre in Coalville
A walk or car ride down the hill.

We found a Costa, had a chat
Discussed our options while we sat.
We travelled back a different route
A pleasant drive, a short commute.

Final Decision

So Hinckley's where we want to be
A lovely home for Malc and me.
We now know that we want a flat
A time for us is where we're at.

A long time now we didn't know
Should we stay or should we go.
Our family home it's always been
It's too big now, too much to clean.

We love our home, there is no doubt
But now it's time to move on out.
We've loved it here for sixteen years
Have known some joy and shed some tears.

So six of us there used to be
But some moved out, and now we're three.
We're older now so we must do
Things we enjoy, some old some new.

Flickering Light

And then there was a dark dark place
With all the hell you had to face.
You think this time can never end
So much is broken it won't mend.

And somehow as you battle on
When all your hope and strength has gone.
You pass a day, a night, a week
When rest and sleep is all you seek.

You're in a tunnel stretching far
Not knowing who or what you are.
You trudge along the blackened space
No start or end, it's not a race.

So in a circle, round and round
Your feet smash on the stony ground.
Your eyes adjust but still no light
You're cold and lost. You have no fight.

So IS this all that's meant to be
A spiral of black agony.
You can't go forward, can't go back
Around and round the same old track.

But then there's light, well just a chink
You walk towards it, dare not blink.
The light grows bigger, then it's gone
Shall you give up or struggle on.

You're in the car. A sunny day.
The music plays. You're on our way.
You see a lady frail and worn
And ponder as you are reborn.

What is her story? Can she see
The spiral of black agony?
You've done your sentence. Now you're free.
To walk the path of bravery.

Full of Beans

Full of Beans is the place to eat
Where Val will greet you. Take a seat.
Brekkie is served until midday
Go and buy yours without delay.

They just do a great panini
Served up by their own food genie.
Fresh espresso, one shot or two
Plus herbal teas and tea cakes too.

Various soups with crusty bread
A choice of white or brown instead.
Handmade cakes are so delightful
Wanting more with every biteful.

Try their yummy chunky baguettes
These are just as good as it gets.
Toasties, coleslaw and pasta bakes
Coffee, teas and a choice of cakes.

This little cafe is such a gem
With lots of banter and mayhem.
Full of Beans is a happy place
In Galley Common. Show your face.

Glad to Be Me

I used to wish I could be you
Always so poised and pretty too.
Your confidence was oozing out
And I was shy and full of doubt.

Your mum and you were so well dressed
Where mine was shabby and depressed.
I couldn't even talk to you
So different to the world I knew.

I used to think it wasn't fair
That normal people roamed out there.
My gorgeous cousin one of them
Her life seemed calm without mayhem.

I got older and saw her less
My life was hard with lots of stress.
My children were the world to me
I made a home. Our sanctuary.

My cousin had a girl and boy
A husband too to bring her joy.
I heard the wait was hard and long
To hear those cries. A mother's song.

One day my sister came to me
And told me of a tragedy.
A man had died whilst having fun
She said it was my cousin's son.

Her young son gone! Still in his prime!
A life to live! But no more time!
The quarry where he met his friends
Stands mocking as this young life ends.

I saw my cousin. Lovely still.
The same calm face she had until
She spoke about that fateful day
Her grieving eyes gave much away.

Then as her words would come no more
She wore the face she had before.
Her comfort blanket used to hide
The deepest pain she feels inside.

I said goodbye and felt so sad
And thought about the life I'd had.
So glad that wishes don't come true
That I'm still me and you're still you.

Grandbaby Day

Give me a second I used to say
As I began my grannie day
A day off work, a chance to see
A bit more of my family.

Excited children, tales to tell
"Grannie, Grannie," they would yell.
Try to listen, hear each word
Half a sentence is all I heard.

Waiting to catch every letter
Maybe this week I'll do better.
Ready to listen, Alfie first
The other two are fit to burst.

Teddie's upset, he wants to talk
Millie is saying she wants to walk.
Alfie is chatting, lots of news
Things to say, no time to lose.

Give me a second I used to say
But somehow that won't work today.
Try to search for gloves or phone
"You're not listening," the kiddies groan

Grandma's House

We'd found a house. A house we'd love
So warm and snug. A cosy glove.
Now it was time to make a move
Remove the needle from the groove.

It was our home for many years
We raised our kids. Shared love and tears.
But now there's only me and you
A fresh new start. Begin anew.

Decision made. We looked ahead
He wanted it! Our buyer said!
A chapter closed. A brand-new start
With memories padlocked in my heart.

We made appointments. Four to view
We'd see them in a day or two.
A little window caught my eye
A fifty pence against the sky.

The bathroom with its hexagon
This love affair had just begun.
We didn't view the other three
This was the place we had to be.

So it was ours and we moved in
A private garden! What a win.
A sunny space with lots of trees
I sit and feel the gentle breeze.

The house is perfect and so calm
Protecting us from stress and harm.
"It's Grandma's house," my grandkids say
It takes me to a distant day.

A time a place where I could be
Accepted, loved just being me.
My grandma's house when I was young
The games we played, the songs we sung.

So in the autumn of our lives
Our kids are grown. Our marriage thrives.
We're living under Grandma's wing
Just as I did back in the spring.

Handful of Dreams

A child's face. The wanderlust
Eyes looking up, so full of trust.
Not asking for the sun or moon
But just a shiny green balloon.

The adult says, "No, not today
No money left for us to pay."
There are so many, tied with string
"Just five pound each," we hear him sing.

They bob about so bright and free
Can someone find a home for me?
"Please Mum, can I just have one?"
She's looking back, we travel on.

Some years have passed since you last cried
And looked at me with eyes so wide.
With hope that I might change my mind
You'd asked again, then looked behind.

I never knew how much you yearned
Though now I know and I have learned.
It would have meant the world to you
To hold that string so shining new.

An illness that was quite severe
Just filled us all with dread and fear.
You came back home to rest and mend
Tea, cake and chat, a girl's best friend.

I asked you could you close your eyes
As I had you a nice surprise.
You held the string and then you saw
What you had missed when you were four.

I saw the face I'd seen before
So full of wanderlust and awe.
The happiness denied before
Was now all hers at twenty-four.

Hear Me!

You may not know that I misheard
I lost the meaning, missed a word.
You look at me, I seem annoyed
I look around, I'm in a void.

I want to shout, "I can't take part!"
I can't express what's in my heart.
I'm hopeful that you'll understand
My muffled ruffled silent land.

I'm isolated in frustration
Victim of my segregation.
I'm angry and I'm so alone
Can't hear my voice, can't check my tone.

A social evening, it's a test
Just look at me, I'm so depressed.
I can't join in, missed what you said
Too many noises in my head.

I'm sitting here nowhere to hide
Makes me think of suicide
I'm so embarrassed, so worn down
I can't join in. A party clown.

Throughout the years I've missed so much
Relying more on smell, sight, touch.
There's so much anger locked inside
That when I cry, I'm open wide.

I hear your voice! I hear it new!
For fifteen years I've not known you!
I can hear that paper rustle
Over all the morning bustle!

I grip your hand and start to cry
So many noises rushing by.
Waiting to cross I hear the beep
I've woken up. I've been asleep.

The world is softer but so crisp
The noises come. I start to drift.
I ask you, "Can you hear that bird?"
You smile and say you hadn't heard.

It's noisy but it's great to me
I pick out different sounds you see.
Someone laughs. An engine starts.
Sounds shoot at me like target darts.

I've missed so much. You squeeze my hand.
You share with me my wonderland.
I'm happy now. I'll start anew
Dr Monksfield, a huge THANK YOU!

I hear the music. Now I'll dance.
As I've been given one more chance
To enjoy life and wear a smile
To sit and hear. To wait a while.

Homeless

A teenage girl, a swelling tum
At college now, but soon a mum.
Friday lessons over and done
The long walk home has just begun.

Twelve hours pass, her son is born
A brand-new life, a brand-new dawn.
Her sister waits to take a look
A photo for her picture book.

She's homeless now, her mum said "No"
She can't go home, nowhere to go.
What happens now? She's filled with fear
She holds her boy and sheds a tear.

Hubby

Oh darling, I do love you
You're the only one for me.
You found my lonely heart at last
And entered with a key.

I know I'll never let you out
Such things I cannot do.
Especially as I've locked you in
So no one can get through.

You found my heart and came inside
Not sure if you could stay.
You looked around, we fell in love
I threw the key away.

If ever I did let you out
My heart would have to break.
And then once more reality
Would dawn when I awake.

I Am an Orphan

I am an orphan, my parent's gone
No mum, no dad, I'm classed as one.
It took a while to face the truth
As they were there throughout my youth.

It's Father's Day, no card to buy
They're in the shops, I want to cry.
I've handed my last card to Dad
The realisation makes me sad.

It's Mother's Day, again the same
No card to buy, can't sign my name.
Next year I said, I will be strong
But March, then June, just proved me wrong.

I'm Always There

This job I have is not for me
My friends just bore me constantly.
I'm getting fed up of my street
Ignoring neighbours that I meet.

I would be happy somewhere new
I'll move away, that's what I'll do.
I will escape, jump on a bus
And leave behind chaos and fuss.

I've made a brand-new plan today
Just leave it all and run away.
I can't be happy while I'm here
I'll pack my bags and disappear.

A brand-new house, a shiny door
Things looking better than before.
Hot chocolate and some bread and jam
I go to bed and THERE I AM.

A bright new start, a brand-new view
But every day I'LL BE THERE TOO.
I've made my problems history
But when alone there's ONLY ME!

And so, I've travelled far and wide
I look behind nowhere to hide.
Wherever I run to THERE I'LL BE.
My day begins and ends with ME!

It Will Be OK

I've done it wrong again today!
"Don't worry, it will be OK."
Why can't I always get it right!
The same thoughts coming back to bite!

That was a stupid thing to say!
"Don't worry it will be OK."
Must work faster! Get it done!
Just lighten up and have some fun!

Today is looking dull and grey
"Don't worry it will be OK."
Just be polite! Be extra nice!
Make sure you're giving good advice.

I need to put more stock away!
"Don't worry it will be OK."
But first I'll put these tickets out!
"Sue can you serve?" I hear her shout!

The RFL is low today!
"Don't worry it will be OK."
He didn't want to have a card!
Perhaps I shouldn't try so hard!

I need five minutes if I may
"Don't worry it will be OK."
Take another for half price
Please and thank you, must be nice.

This little voice my self esteem
Breaks through my thoughts as if a dream.
I'll listen to that voice tonight
Tomorrow it should be alright.

Tomorrow comes I stand and smile
I need to go that extra mile.
"Please, is this in the penny sale?"
"It's not on now," I stand and wale!

Jade

The day you lost your lovely sister
Had you hugged and had you kissed her.
I heard the news! I could have cried!
Such mixed emotions deep inside.

Thinking that I didn't like you
I judged you as we often do.
And coming from that side of town
Where people tend to look and frown.

You seemed so cold and self-assured
A face that said I'm posh and bored.
But home was Mum, who liked to drink
A younger sis, with you their link.

At fourteen Chelsea lost her life
It pierced my heart just like a knife.
You were a family. Three of you.
You shared your life. And now there's two.

I'm thinking back, when we were three
With my two girls, a family.
Not much money, but lots of love
Your lovely sister rests above.

Her young life spent – a poorly heart
With family struggles from the start.
The day she had her surgery
It broke apart your team of three.

I saw your strength. It changed my view.
I changed the way I looked at you.
A little mum you must have been
So grown up for a little teen.

I think about my girls and me
That we have kept our team of three.
I think of you. It breaks my heart
That you had such a hard, sad start.

Some months had passed, more than a few
I saw you and I spoke to you.
You're doing well. We talked. We smiled.
But still inside, that broken child!

Jigsaw

Is there a bit that doesn't fit?
Or one piece missing, where is it?
Without the one that's gone astray
It is no good. Throw it away.

The puzzle just cannot survive
It needs each piece to be alive.
It's not complete. It is no use
When joining parts start to come loose.

Each one supports his friend next door
A solid structure ever more.
It will not fit if one piece strays
A careless knock as Johnny plays.

You can't replace that missing piece
The harmony begins to cease.
There is no beauty, just a hole.
The picture's lost its heart and soul.

The jigsaw will be put away
To sleep. No more to shine and play.
The story's gone and incomplete
It's meaning lost in sad retreat.

The sadness of the broken team
No more to smile or reign supreme.
The glory of the unique bits
Lights up as each one neatly fits.

Come on let's all stick together
Battle on despite the weather.
Each one caring for their neighbour
An act of loving, never labour.

Karen

I've been divorced for many years
After shedding lots of tears.
Trapped in a marriage of pure hell
I told the kids, "We'll go, we shall."

Where would we stay, I did not know
We didn't have a place to go.
But then an angel did appear
And said to me, "You can stop here."

She put us up all five of us
Without a second thought or fuss.
My lovely sis, a heart of gold
When they made her, they broke the mould.

Her lovely home she opened wide
So we could all stay safe inside.
She changed my life, she set us free
The kindest angel there could be.

Lacey

Lacey you are a special girl
More precious than a jewel or pearl.
You always smile, you make us glad
You cheer us up when we are sad.

You are so clever and pretty too
No one dances as good as you.
We love your acro, you're the best
We love you North, South, East and West.

Lady Isobel

The restaurant where we first met
Her name I never will forget.
She was so striking all in red
And very poised from toe to head.

She looked at us with great intent
So still and truly elegant.
They called her Lady Isobel
Where was she from? We couldn't tell.

The introduction at our table
Made us feel a bit unstable.
We'd never met her type before
Not speaking, as we were in awe.

Could she dine with us? We were asked
We both sat there a bit aghast!
"Why not! Sure!" we finally said.
"Great. Would you like some garlic bread?"

Then he took Isobel away
"We'll be back soon," he turned to say.
"It will be fine," Malc said to me
"She's bright and fresh, if not friendly!"

She came back, but not so dapper
Not so much the cool red snapper.
Although she'd come back in disguise
There's no mistake those staring eyes.

She joined us so that we could dine
An eye on Malc's plate, one on mine.
We flipped her over. Saw the red.
An eyeball each and half her head!

Let's Play

There is a way we should behave
The social graces are our slave.
We smile. We laugh. We just agree
Who are they sitting next to me!

I see the people filing in
Terror hidden behind a grin.
A mental note of who is there
Avoid their gazes just don't stare.

If I don't look, perhaps they'll go
Find someone they already know.
I grab my bag and look inside
The empty chair begins to slide.

The dreaded echoes of a voice
I smile of course, I have no choice.
Perhaps she'll faint or change her mind
Oh, am I mad or just unkind.

"Can I sit here?" she says to me
No go away and set me free!
Don't want to chat and be polite
I force a smile with all my might.

"Of course you can," I falsely say
The first impression? Drab and grey!
We exchange names and fix our eyes
The truth that can't disguise the lies.

I think she felt the same as me
An evening of uncertainty.
Shall we go home and watch TV
Better than this reality!

The social norm as people say
Shall we play it again today.
We'll laugh and chat try not to shout.
"Bloody hell, what's this all about!"

Ling Mell

I stand before the strange front door
Where I'd been four decades before.
So much had changed in all that time
My Aunt and Uncle in their prime.

I didn't know it, though I should
A winding road down to a wood.
And in my head the ghostly sounds
As memories float and swim around.

My cousins were so young back then
I babysat them way back when.
My memories were so vague, I tried
To picture them and me inside.

I hear the slamming of the door
High heels clonking on the floor.
I sit upright. The children sleep
I'm woken from a dream so deep.

My Auntie's voice is loud and shrill
I'm wide awake and then until
The clock says three. They go to bed.
Their words are buzzing in my head!

The house is dark, I'm in the car
I can't believe we've come this far.
A lifetime's passed as I stand here
Can all those years just disappear?

Louise

"Something's not right," you said to me
As we walked from maternity.
It's six o'clock, a cold dark night
I tell you it will be alright.

The scan reveals too much water
I start to worry for my daughter.
The midwife said, "We need a date
That's not too early or too late."

The day arrived for babe to come
Some flowers and a "Thank you, Mum."
I'd come to mind my two grandsons
I told them that I loved them tons.

I had a call. It wasn't good.
Things had gone wrong I understood.
A waiting game all through the night
I prayed my daughter be alright.

The waiting room in ITU
We sat and cried and prayed for Lou.
My eldest daughter by my side
Dreading the news that Lou had died.

You had a relapse in the night
But strong enough to win the fight.
The night was over. You pulled through.
We saw you and we spoke to you.

You were asleep all bruised and pale
So lucky but so weak and frail.
We spoke to you of Alf and Ted
You have a girl we gently said.

An AFE. It's very rare.
That night the midwife was aware.
She saw the signs and acted fast
Lifesaving speed as seconds passed.

When we drive by maternity
I hear those words you said to me.
That place in time will always be
A very poignant memory.

We rallied round that Christmas time
A festive day spent out of rhyme.
A mum and sister for the boys
A family saved, plus lots of toys.

Madeira

We found our slice of paradise
Each year to visit, once or twice.
A lovely sunny place to go
With faces new, and some we know.

So Funchal is our favourite place
Walking down at a steady pace.
We sit outside and have a drink
Some time to stare, relax and think.

Our favourite place we love to sit
Where we can gaze and rest a bit.
The pan pipes play their melody
This is the place I like to be.

Mother's Day

I'm feeling loved, I have to say
I've had a lovely Mother's Day.
So many cards, and pressies too
Flowers from Nic, a bag from Lou.

Mugs from Doop, vouchers from Jay
And from Lee, Ferroro Rocher.
I had a lovely handmade card
How did he do it? Was it hard?

So out for brekkie we did go
To Tarro Lounge. Oh no, no, no!
The place was full! There was a queue
So now what are we meant to do!

To Sutton Cheney we set out
That would be full, there was no doubt!
We found a space! We parked the car!
It's looking good. Well good so far.

So to the cafe we did go
Yes! Empty tables, five or so.
We found a table in the sun
So Mother's Day had just begun.

Moving On

I love my job but I get tired
So is it time that I retired.
I think about it now and then
So now it's just a case of when.

Would I get bored when stuck at home
From room to room would I just roam.
There seems so many things to do
The hours we have are very few.

Maybe I'm just assessing things
Is this what getting older brings.
Moving house is the place to start
With some of our stuff we must part.

We need to have a good clear out
Good for the soul there is no doubt.
We'll hire a skip and fill it high
With stuff we didn't need to buy.

Then we will put our house for sale
Then moving forward, we can't fail.
To change our lives and simplify
These major things as time goes by.

Nic

I can't believe you're twenty-nine
When you were born, you were all mine.
As you grew up, I had to share
To let you go, but still to care.

I've always been so proud of you
Of who you are and what you do.
You got a job. Earned a degree.
You tamed your dogs and won Hestie.

Today is such a special day
I've caught the train, I'm on my way.
To have a chat and drink some tea
Some catch up time, just you and me.

Nicola

My daughter's gone to A and E
Taken from work they said to me.
What can be wrong. I need to know
We're in the car and off we go.

She's crying and her make-up's run
Oh no what's wrong! What had she done!
I cuddled her. She clung to me
What had happened! What could it be!

She tries to speak. She makes some sounds.
I see her fear as my heart pounds.
I'm frightened as I talk to her
I want things as they were before.

I hug her and she looks at me
I ask her very gently
"Do you know what you want to say?"
She looks relieved and nods away.

Her eyes are speaking clear to me
She needs my help to set her free.
"Your words are jumbled, do you know?"
Her eyes are wide as tears flow.

She's nodding and I love her so
She's very poorly we both know.
They find a clot within her brain
I couldn't let her see my pain.
They thinned her blood and stopped the bleed

And sleep was all she seemed to need
We told her she must stay awake
Eyes telling, "I'm tired, I need a break."

As days go by, you're on the mend
You worried me I can't pretend.
Your speech improved, you spoke to me
Then finally you were set free.

It had been hard to hide my tears
To hide from you my deepest fears.
I couldn't accept that you might die
I took some time and had a cry.

Nightmare of Dreams

I said, "Let's go and see Grandma
She really doesn't live that far."
So in the car, all set to go
She's moved away! Of course I know!

I told my friend, and then I said
"What am I doing, Grandma's dead!"
"Just love me," someone said to me
I couldn't move. Who could it be.

I tried to wake, open my eyes
I woke but lay there paralysed.
My friend was laying in my bed
I shouted, but inside my head.

Lay in my bed nowhere to hide
I wake and find I haven't died.
I know someone is next to me
I couldn't move to try and see.

I couldn't move. I couldn't shout
I knew my words weren't coming out.
I felt so sad. I need her here
And right away she did appear.

She's taking me I realised
I cried because I knew she'd died.
I said, "It's not my time to go."
I told her I still loved her so.

I said, "I'm needed here on earth."
Trying to wake for all I'm worth.
I see the room though still asleep
I close my eyes then have a peep.

So now I know I AM awake
But I can't move for goodness sake.
Waking, sleeping, it's all the same
I've had enough of this mad game!

I said, "It's not my time to go."
My grandma knows I love her so.
I said goodbye, she smiled and waved
I knew for now I had been saved.

Ninety Minutes

We didn't mean to buy that day
Out for a walk, we passed your way.
Looking for Tom, just to say "Hi."
He wasn't in, so we walked on by.

A lady came out and said "Hello"
Was Tom around, did she know?
She confirmed that he wasn't there
Started to chat about time share.

Our slot was booked, his name was Steve
Ninety minutes then we could leave.
We saw the plans and had some tea
Were shown two rooms and saw the sea.

Steve was great, he sold it well
He knew his stuff and how to sell.
So genuine and friendly too
Champagne, chat and a huge

THANK YOU.

No Relief

And what's this! A water infection
I won't accept it, I choose rejection.
Trips to the loo, drinking lots of water
Cut the severity by a quarter.

Need a wee can't wait any longer
Sit on the loo, the feelings stronger.
Just no relief whatever I do
I'll sit here with a book or two.

Old Age

Your home care is where it will end
You won't get well, we can't pretend.
Your independence you fought for
To live inside your own front door.

Your lovely home so clean and neat
The proudest lady I could meet.
Your left arm is no good to you
But even so you've made it through.

You live alone, you've had some falls
But you remain inside YOUR walls.
You're weaker now. The carers come.
I hope they know you're someone's mum!

Your lovely skin, those eager eyes
You are aware, you're still so wise.
You had no help, but you were tired
You are someone I have admired.

Equipment dotted everywhere
As you accept your full-time care.
A great grandma you have become
We hold the baby on your tum.

Your calming voice. That soothing tone.
He wriggles then a moan and groan.
He looks at you with eyes so wide
He listens and his cries subside.

The young and old at peace as one
Just love and pleasure, all pain gone.
The years between them just skin deep
Contented breath. He goes to sleep.

Paradise Found

Madeira is the place to be
The people here are so friendly.
Levada walks and mountain tours
Much too pretty to stay indoors.

The flowers bloom, the sun is out
What isn't there to shout about.
Good service given everywhere
The people here just seem to care.

Taxi drivers, cleaners too
Take great pride in what they do.
Sweet music plays from every place
And life, for now, is not a race.

Princess

Everything is such a drama!
Try to be a little calmer.
You really put yourself to shame
When you point your finger of blame!

You have a way to twist the truth
And make up things when there's no proof.
So are you part of this great team?
No not to me it does not seem!

You pull the wool and laugh and joke
My hidden anger makes me choke.
You're crafty, selfish through and through
I want to scream and shout at you!

The customer comes first you know
But you're the princess of your show.
Your till's the stage where you parade
Please put your bushel in the shade!

As supervisor you should be
A great example totally.
You do not lead or motivate
Chaos, commotion you create!

We know you have a baby bump
In front of you a growing lump.
You must take time to rest and eat
And take the weight from off your feet.

But please don't milk it, take the pee
We know you have a pregnancy.
To take your leave I know you yearn
And when you do, please don't return!

Rachel and Us

We thought that mobile would be best
Just stay at home and have a rest.
With both our hairs done together
Stay indoors, forget the weather.

Loubie has the kids to sort out
A mobile's best there is no doubt
Haircut and dyed, the kids can play
Us girlies have our pamper day.

I searched on google, tried a few
Got a reply from one or two.
One was full, the other was free
Who found a gap for Lou and me.

Her name was Rachel, she was great
We didn't have too long to wait.
She saw us both within a week
Nice and bubbly, she loved to speak.

She's done our hair for many years
We've laughed and joked and shed some tears.
She is a friend, she knows us well
We all get on, we seem to gel.

She knows the way we like our hair
She gets it right, she seems to care.
Her baby's due in a month or so
On maternity leave she must go.

She booked us in close to her date
Then after that, eight weeks to wait.
Please baby come when you are due
We don't mind, just a day or two.

So Rachel, you are just the best
Much better than all the rest.
I'll come to you if I really must
You're the hairdresser we can trust.

Rain!

Here's the rain! Well, I can feel it!
It's in the air! There's quite a bit!
Windscreens dry, but my brolley's out
I felt some drops, there is no doubt!

Into Sainsburys. Purse out to pay.
The young man asked, "Had a good day?"
He was pleasant and so jolly
Then he spotted my dry brolley!

"Is it raining?" He looked outside.
He couldn't see it though he tried.
"It's just started. It's in the air."
I saw him squint and start to stare.

"I see it now," he said at last.
I knew it wasn't coming fast.
"I'm keeping dry," I brightly said.
I scurried out and clutched my bread!

Seasons for a Reason

The pom-pom on the woolly hat
Pulled down around a golden plait.
A sunny day, the wind is strong
As days grow shorter, nights are long.

The leaves are dropping, people walk
Holding hands, they laugh and talk.
Passing the wharf, a narrowboat
Canoeists, ducks and swans afloat.

The coffee tables placed outside
With many more set out inside.
It's blowing but the sun is warm
The clouds are whipping up a storm.

Sit by the water, take a chair
Not many people sitting there.
It's peaceful as the boats go by
A coffee and a chocolate pie.

I love the seasons, scarves and coats
The winter walks, the painted boats.
I like the summer, autumn too
It's great when spring pops into view.

So which to choose, the frost, the sun?
The snow, the rain, which is most fun?
The wind, the storms, the clouds, the gales
The fog, the mist or maybe hail?

Choose woolly hats or swimming suits
Umbrellas, flip flops, shorts or boots.
Let's wear them all! We'll just rotate!
There really isn't long to wait.

I love winter, the log fire's on
Then it's spring, the snow has gone.
Summer comes, the sun warms me through
The autumn grass spread thick with dew.

Slowing Down

A week ago, it was the day
My husband said he'd run away.
Was overwhelmed, he couldn't cope
No joy. No love. No sign of hope.

I felt so helpless, full of fear
He'd run away and disappear.
Then shouting he was really mad
He didn't want the life we had.

He felt unloved and pushed aside
Nowhere to turn. Nowhere to hide.
"Listen to me!" he firmly said
His anger buzzing in my head.

I felt so sick throughout the day
Too many years to throw away.
I felt so tired, just need a way
To trample through these clouds of grey.

Accepting things the way they are
Open your mind up just ajar.
If you do that then you will see
A way to do things differently.

I thought about what you had said
And rolled it round inside my head.
We're both so busy in the day
So many things get in the way.

We must make time for you and me
So much to say, so much to see.
We should slow down, it's time to say
Let's have a calmer richer day.

I've cut my hours, you've cut yours too
I think about the job you do.
Clippers to clean, and notes to file
Cards to pull, and numbers to dial.

That awful day, I thought you'd go
When both of us were really low.
It helped us face what had to change
Our life style had a re-arrange.

Starting Over

This lonely place, low self esteem
To feel equal would be a dream.
To give a child a sense of worth
A parent's job right from their birth.

To feel you are a waste of space
And think you have an ugly face.
That everyone is better than you
To have no belief in what you do.

To feel that you are all alone
"What's wrong with you," my dad would groan.
Negative comments, they will stick
"Sue is pretty, but she is thick."

I never felt I fitted in
And day by day I couldn't win.
I always thought I'd never be
Acceptable, just being me.

If only I'd felt good enough
To just get through the daily stuff.
It weighs you down, it rules your life
Just adding to your woes and strife.

A small child learns what he is told
By the time he is five years old.
When you are angry, choose each word
"What's wrong with you?" is what I heard.

No smiling face. No hugs from Mum
Please talk to me, don't look so glum.
You think you have done something wrong
When she ignores you all day long.

You can work on your self-belief
And feel the ripples of relief.
Re-tune your mind and start anew
A brand-new start! A brand-new you!

The Chemist

We didn't think we'd last this long
When early on it all went wrong.
He couldn't love me, though he tried
Six months after Elaine had died.

He was still grieving for his wife
For fifteen years she was his life.
With two small boys, the youngest seven
Knowing their mum had gone to heaven.

What he told me then, I could tell
He had been through a living hell.
His wife had died so suddenly
Seeking advice, he came to me.

His boys weren't eating, nor was he
Could I suggest a remedy.
A single parent I was too
And knew what he was going through.

His concern was plain to see
I offered him my sympathy.
A multivit he took to try
He thanked me and then said goodbye.

He came to the shop a few times more
A genuine man is what I saw.
Hurt and lost, but reaching out
I did like him, there was no doubt.

Sometime after that first meeting
We met by chance, a lovely greeting.
He quickly wrote his number down
Brightened up my trip to town.

The Closed Door

I'll keep it closed, at least today
You've left and now you're on your way.
Back to the world you call your home
Your day by day, your free to roam.

We've had a spell of yours and mine
Our separate lives join and combine.
You're in my world that once was yours
You left and opened many doors.

You are familiar with my life
The ups and downs, the woes the strife.
You moved away and started new
A city life, a brand-new you.

The room I use to store some things
With all the clutter that it brings
Was cleared away, restored anew
Cleaned and ready to welcome you.

You caught your train and came to us
Time to forget the prep and fuss.
With cuddles and a welcome smile
A cuppa and then chat a while.

The break is over, time to go
I'm sad and then I feel so low.
Their room stays closed behind the door
Until again it is a store.

Tomorrow is another day
Today I think I'll stay away.
Don't want to look, don't want to see
The room I'd cleaned dull and lonely.

The Empty Bag

So anger plays a part you see
And is inside of you and me.
We can deny it, keep it down
Then force a smile and wear a frown.

Throughout the years of joy and pain
We wipe our tears and start again.
Then wear a face that's proud and strong
It starts to crack! It's all gone wrong.

You've made some friends along the way
But don't care where they are today.
A strategy to get you by
You're tired of it but don't know why.

The past creeps back, it says I'm here
Reminds you of the things you fear.
A lot of pain so deep inside
It couldn't find a place to hide.

It pops up waving, "Here I am!"
Pretending you don't give a damn.
The past is saying, "Look at me
Yes, I am your reality."

A self-help book. A place to start
The words within can heal your heart.
Addiction! No! That isn't me.
So now I'm off the hook you see.

Don't need the book. I'm off to bed
With "PEOPLE PLEASER" in my head!
I lay there and I start to dream
I've dropped and lost my self-esteem.

I make a cuppa. See the book
It might be worth another look.
I don't take drugs or overdrink
But now I think there is a link.

My weary pen begins to write
The truth about my new insight.
I jot down all the people who
Throughout my life have made me blue.

I feel the anger, write a list
Then checking there's no one I've missed.
I now have movement in my bag
It's full! It makes my shoulder sag!

As one by one I let them out
I face each one and freely shout.
"YOU MADE ME ANGRY! NOW I'M FREE!"
I throw my bag. It's now empty.

The House

The house stands still! So tall and proud!
Its silence conceals a noisy crowd.
Across the street, it stands upright
Awake all day. Asleep all night.

The house keeps watch, it sees it all!
The doorbell sounds around the hall.
The silence expends towards the door
It spills around the walls and floor.

The curtains open, there's life inside!
The door unlocks, it opens wide.
The house wakes up. It's warm and bright
Packed with love and stuffed with light.

Unmoving it remains the same!
It stands determined! Hides the shame!
Returning home, they're sucked inside!
The house provides a place to hide!

The Makeshift Home

The old man shuffles slowly by
He's so unkempt I wonder why
Who does he have to love and care
To see he has clean clothes to wear.

He's slowly coming down the hill
The same old clothes he'll wear until
The day he dies, and if he's found
Will he be missed when not around?

Where is this place he calls his home?
He comes and goes, he's free to roam.
A makeshift shed, a numbered door
A letter box we clearly saw??

The Party Dress

It's funny when you are a child
Your mum and dad can drive you wild.
I never could get close to Mum
No hugs from her, she looked so glum.

When I was home, she didn't speak
What's wrong with me, am I a freak?
I used to please as best I could
I'd upset Mum. I wasn't good.

As I grew up, I felt the shame
It wasn't me, Mum was to blame!
I felt so angry and deprived.
But then I thought, 'I have survived!'

Soon my anger turned to sorrow
I would live a new tomorrow.
Where I could feel my mother's pain
A lonely life, spent in the rain.

It makes me sad, I want to cry.
I wish I could have asked her why.
She always pushed our love away
"Did she need us?" I asked one day.

She looked at me, and then she cried
Sat in her bed right by my side.
She looked so small. I loved her so.
She answered "Yes," I felt a glow.

I felt I knew her for a while
To feel the love and see the smile.
She needed me. She looked so scared.
From that day on I knew she cared.

I look back now and see the love
I thank her as I look above.
For all the things she did for me
And now I know I am set free.

The party dress I loved so much
Picked for me with a mother's touch.
The birthday parties every year
The cake I see. The joy I hear.

Some memories I cannot replace
Like waking in a magic place.
Upon our beds so neatly laid
Clothes for our dolls that Mum had made.

The Steady Fare

Taxi drivers everywhere
Hoping soon to get a fare.
Stood in groups they have a chat
A laugh, a joke, a friendly pat.

Not quite light but they are out
They know what earning's all about.
They calmly stand throughout the day.
A fare or two to pay their way.

They look so happy, cheerful too
The yellow cabs look bright and new.
The men blend in as I look down
I see the shops, the sea the town.

Tightrope

We walk a tightrope through our life
As sharp and deadly as a knife.
A careless move. A quick remark
A lifetime's memories in the dark!

The circus act, mouths open wide
They're in the air, nowhere to hide.
The show will end. The danger gone
But your tightrope goes on and on!

Start in the middle. Keep it there
Lean left. Lean right. You're in despair!
You cannot stop. Look straight ahead
See hard decisions. Some you dread.

A mother treads this lonely line
Devoid of clues. Not one clear sign.
A careless word. A thoughtless act
Your child will feel the full impact.

You make a label. It will stick
Prepare it, but before you lick.
It will bond fast, so do you want
Your child to wear this monument.

So many choices everyday
What chores to do, what games to play.
An empty book for you to fill
Create a life mould at your will.

A wise mum knows they are a team
Today's lesson, build self-esteem.
She has to learn along the way
What not to do, what not to say.

A damaged child will soon grow up
What has she gathered in her cup?
She'll pick it up and drink it down
It's bitter! And she wears a frown.

Each day's a struggle she must win
She'll smile and let the day begin.
Wearing her labels everyday
She tore them off. Threw them away.

HER children wear no tell-tale tag!
NO bags of dark for them to drag.
SHE cultivated self esteem
A cupcake life. Their smile the CREAM!

View from a Balcony

The lady with the sweeping brush
She sweeps the leaves, not in a rush
She glances up at passers by
A lovely day, a clear blue sky.

The leaves have gone, the path is clear
A new leaf drops, a few appear.
She's working hard, her mind is calm
I love it here, each plant, each palm.

What, No Tele!

What, no tele! How can that be!
No BBC or ITV!
No channel five or channel four
No Jezza or Judge Rinder's Law.

No Bradley Walsh or Dragon's Den!
No Country File or News at Ten!
No sitting down to watch Location!
That's because we're on vacation!

Where Do You Want to Live Today?

Where do you want to move today?
Round the corner or far away?
Over the road or down the hill?
At the top of an old windmill?

Stoney Stanton or Hinckley town
A maisonette. Live up or down?
A mobile home. A caravan?
Any for sale? Ask the man.

In the country or by the sea?
Where is it that you want to be?
Skeggy, Bournemouth or Leicester Square?
Oxford Street, Park Lane or Mayfair?

A flat, a house, a garden shed?
Shall we follow our heart or head?
A narrowboat and live the dream?
Not as simple as it may seem.

Stay where we are or move away?
Where do we want to live today?
Sell the house and live by the sea?
Where is it that we want to be?

Wiola

A London show. A happy day.
It's mostly dry though skies are grey.
A breakfast, then a river cruise
The menu now. It's time to choose.

A glass of wine. It starts to rain.
We've had the starters. Now the main.
The sun comes out. We have our pudd.
A chocolate slice. It tastes so good.

A train, a boat and then a bus
We're having fun the six of us.
A show, and we're all taking part
So you're a spade, and I'm a heart.

A fairy tale from years gone by
The babies fight, and then they fly.
Who stole the tarts, the queen had made!
The diamonds point! It was a spade!

A looking glass. A young girl's face.
And then she's gone, without a trace.
She's falling up. She's climbing high.
As all her dreams just pass her by.

A fantasy! Reality!
And then it's all mixed up you see!
She's fallen down the rabbit hole.
And can't get out. She's lost her soul.

She Holds Your Hand

You and your mum, you share a name
I look at you, you look the same.
Her pretty face, and lovely hair
A life together, love to share.

You loved her, and she loved you too
Was always there to care for you.
A little girl for her to hold
To love and hug, a pot of gold.

So many days of joy and fun
A mother's love had just begun.
She watched you grow, so full of pride
Your life's adventure, side by side.

The bond you had will never die
As you remember years gone by.
When you could walk, she held your hand
She steadied you and let you stand.

We always think of things we'd say
If we could just have one more day.
Have no regrets. Embrace the past.
The memories made will always last.

Your mum will know what's in your heart
She's been with you right from the start.
Just close your eyes and feel her there
A mother's love beyond compare.

As life moves on throughout the years
You will not shed so many tears.
You'll think of her and you will smile
She held your hand for a short while.

So as you start a brand-new day
Your mum will guide you on your way.
She'll pick you up if you should fall
Just like she did when you were small.

Woodpecker Close

A lovely house, a place to share
It doesn't really matter where.
To keep you warm and safe and dry
Your own retreat from eyes that pry.

To be together that's what matters
The smell of food, a saucepan clatters.
Homely sounds of love and laughter
Sing from every beam and rafta.

You Stayed, I Played

When love has died, it's hard to know
Stay where you are, or up and go.
Children depend on mum and dad
Won't leaving now just make them sad.

The arguments that they may see
Or family days spent silently.
Disruptions of a set routine
Would that be kind, or is it mean?

You never really will be sure
You'll leave the house and shut the door.
If you'd have stayed, would things work out?
Don't walk away if there's a doubt.

A child can feel so insecure
To lose the life they had before.
The world can be a scary place
Without the comfort of Dad's face.

I loved it at the end of day
When Dad came home and he would say
"Hello girls, how have you been?"
"What have you done, who have you seen?"

He did leave home eventually
So then we weren't a family.
He would have left some years before
But he chose not to close the door.

I'm glad he stayed and led the way
To make me what I am today.
He taught me all that he held dear
Until he knew this was the year.

Thank you, Dad, for staying longer
Leaving when you felt much stronger.
I'm glad you stayed those extra years
You loved us and you hid your tears.

Mr and Mrs Wood

Karen and Dave now you are wed,
It's time for you to think ahead,
Karen make sure you know your name,
Today it's changed, it's not the same.

You both deserve this special day,
With years of joy to come your way.
So looking forward, moving on,
As your hearts now will beat as one.

I see the love in Karen's eyes,
She's happy now, that's no surprise.
She has a man who loves her so,
You know he does, she wears that glow.

She says, "I am a happy girl,"
"Just look at me, I've found my pearl."
And Dave knows he's a lucky man,
He knew that when their love began.

I must just mention Eleanor,
With her, Dave has a strong rapport.
He takes her out both night and day,
Has Karen's hubby gone astray?

Now in this marriage there are three,
Karen, Dave and a black taxi.
So need a lift? Give Dave a call,
'Cos Woody's Taxi beats them all.

Karen it's great to see you smile,
You've cared for others for a while.
Dave cares for you it's plain to see,
And you love him it's clear to me.

In confidence my sis has grown,
This special man, the best she's known.
So stepping up, we knew Dave 'Wood',
Win Karen's heart and stay for good.

My Shed and Me

The hotel room looked fine to me,
Agreed it had no balcony!
"You would be happy in a shed."
"You'd live in it," you turned and said.

Small but clean and with a sea view,
The furniture they could renew.
Lots of storage for clothes and shoes,
And there's a safe for us to use.

Our valuables, we tucked inside,
We couldn't lock it though we tried.
Never mind, we'll ring downstairs,
Report our problem to repairs.

Later that day hubby despaired,
"When will we get our safe repaired?"
A second call. The man came out,
A click. It's fixed. There was no doubt.

What's that noise? It sounds like drilling,
Oh, it's just our cistern filling.
I had a wash, pulled out the plug,
When will it empty. Glug, glug, glug.

Let's boil the kettle. Time for tea,
Whilst we gaze out and watch the sea.
The room steams up, the switch is stuck,
Oh no we're having such bad luck!

This isn't worth what we have paid,
For all inclusive plus a maid.
"Come on," I say, "let's get some sun."
Our holiday has just begun.

And then a thunderstorm stops play,
Sunbathing finished for today.
We grab our things and run inside,
Back to our room where we get dried.

I COULD be happy in a shed,
It'd be a MANSION in my head.
So would a PALACE set you free?
Just like my little SHED and ME.